SECOND THOUGHTS

FRANK WILLIAM BOREHAM

JOHN BROADBANKS PUBLISHING
EUREKA, CA 2007

John Broadbanks Publishing
Eureka, CA
2007

10 9 8 7 6 5 4 3 2

Printed in the United States of America

ISBN-13 978-0-9790334-2-1
ISBN-10 0-9790334-2-X

Proofreader: Jeff Cranston
Cover Design: Laura Zugzda
Interior Layout: Stephanie Martindale

By the Same Author

Travel Diaries
Loose Leaves (1902)
From England to Mosgiel (1903)

Biography
George Augustus Selwyn (1911)
The Man Who Saved Gandhi
  (1948)

Autobiography
My Pilgrimage (1940)

Essays and Sermons
Won to Glory (1891)
The Whisper of God (1903)
The Luggage of Life (1912)
Mountains in the Mist (1914)
The Golden Milestone (1915)
Mushrooms on the Moor (1915)
Faces in the Fire (1916)
The Other Side of the Hill (1917)
The Silver Shadow (1918)
The Uttermost Star (1919)
A Bunch of Everlastings (1920)
A Reel of Rainbow (1920)
The Home of the Echoes (1921)
A Handful of Stars (1922)
Shadows on the Wall (1922)
Rubble and Roseleaves (1923)
A Casket of Cameos (1924)
Wisps of Wildfire (1924)
The Crystal Pointers (1925)
A Faggot of Torches (1926)
A Tuft of Comet's Hair (1926)
The Nest of Spears (1927)
The Temple of Topaz (1928)

The Fiery Crags (1928)
The Three Half Moons (1929)
The Blue Flame (1930)
When the Swans Fly High (1931)
A Witch's Brewing (1932)
The Drums of Dawn (1933)
The Ivory Spires (1934)
The Heavenly Octave (1935)
Ships of Pearl (1935)
The Passing of John Broadbanks
  (1936)
I Forgot to Say (1939)
The Prodigal (1941)
Boulevards of Paradise (1944)
A Late Lark Singing (1945)
Cliffs of Opal (1948)
Arrows of Desire (1951)
My Christmas Book (1953)
Dreams at Sunset (1954)
In Pastures Green (1954)
The Gospel of Robinson Crusoe
  (1955)
The Gospel of Uncle Tom's Cabin
  (1956)
The Tide Comes In (1958)
The Last Milestone (1961)

Books Published by John Broadbanks Publishing

All the Blessings of Life: The Best
  Stories of F. W. Boreham (2007)
Lover of Life: F. W. Boreham's
  Tribute to His Mentor (2007)
Second Thoughts (2007)

CONTENTS

INTRODUCTION

Of the books that have played the greatest role in molding me, I count many volumes by especially one writer: F. W. Boreham. He authored more than fifty books of essays and pastored congregations in New Zealand, Tasmania, and Australia. He was not the classical preacher—not even a profound, deep preacher—but he was marvelous at seeing beauty in the simple things of life. He heeded John Wesley's charge to young preachers to blend simplicity with sublimity, "the strongest sense in the plainest language."

There are so many of his books that have shaped my thinking—*A Bunch of Everlastings, Boulevards of Paradise*—but perhaps my favorite is *Mushrooms on the Moor*. In his essay of the same name, he whimsically chides G.K. Chesterton (another writer who has greatly influenced me) for not liking, of all things, mushrooms! Yet in his inimitable way, Boreham takes a simple experience of finding mushrooms before dawn and anchors it in a marvelous truth from the Scriptures. "Anybody can grow fine flowers in the daytime," writes Boreham. "But what can you grow in the dark? *That* is the challenge of the mushrooms—*what can you grow in the dark?* The nights are the test! as Charlotte Brontë used to say. They are indeed. Tell me: Can you grow faith, and restfulness, and patience, and a quiet heart in the darkness? If so, you will never speak contemptuously of mushrooms again.

I try to read an essay by Boreham every day to keep myself in tune with life's simple beauties and to not get lost in the complexities of so many other things that my mind is prone to engage. What Boreham once said of another is a fitting endorsement for the reader of his own profound works: "It puts iron into the blood to spend time with one for whom the claim of conscience is supreme and who loves the truth of God with so deathless an affection."

Indeed, each time I have seen new attacks upon the name of Christ, I have drawn much comfort over the years from his beautifully titled essay "The Candle and The Bird" (found in *Boulevards of Paradise*). Boreham observes that God's presence is more analogous to a bird than it is to a candle. When a candle is extinguished, the light goes out. But when a bird is driven away, it only leaves to sing its song on another bough.

With that metaphor in mind Boreham traces the mighty moving of God throughout history. Consider, for example, the impact of the Puritans on their world. As it was waning, Milton bemoaned an England that desperately needed the heart of revival once again. Had the light been extinguished? No, only eight years after the untimely death of Joseph Addison, the highly regarded English Christian statesman, a handful of young people were gathered in prayer at Herrnhut, Germany, on the morning of August 13th, 1727. Led by twenty-seven-year-old Count Zinzendorf, something of enormous import happened. All they could remember was that "they scarcely knew whether they still belonged to the earth or had actually gone to heaven." This was the birth of the Moravian movement. So even as England was becoming barren of a godly influence, the Moravians were raised up in Germany.

From that movement missionaries were sent to the ends of the globe. But then the Moravian movement began to wane. Had the light been extinguished? No, the bird was singing on a different bough. Later in that century it was William Carey who set foot in India, on the very day that the cross was being burned in France. While Voltaire and hostile philosophers had done their work and Europe was breathing threats and slaughter against the gospel, William Carey, with a Bible in one hand and the annals of Moravian Missions in the other, was going to touch the heart of India. And in the dying moments of the Moravian movement, the heart of Wesley was ignited.

But again as the Wesleyan revivals were dying out, had the light been extinguished? No, the bird was singing on a different bough. Inspired by the Puritan thinker Chalmers, W.C. Burns, Alexander Duff, Robert Murray McCheyne, Andrew Bonar and Horatius Bonar were rising to do a work for God in Scotland. And as Scotland saw its heroes fade, suddenly the voice of Charles Haddon Spurgeon rang out from London to thousands at home and abroad. (Interestingly, Boreham himself studied at Spurgeon College and was the last student approved by Spurgeon before the renowned preacher died.)

No, the light is never extinguished. Such is the pattern of "the bird singing its song in different settings." The sun may be setting in one place while rising in another. God's work is always visible somewhere. Like so many of Boreham's essays written years ago, "The Candle and the Bird" concludes with timeless insight for readers worldwide today:

> "When we have occasion to lament the spiritual poverty immediately around us, we may be sure that the bird that has forsaken us is singing his lovely song, to somebody else's rapture, on a distant bough. And so it shall continue until that day dawns for which the Church has ever prayed, when the Holy Dove shall feel equally at home on every shore and the earth shall be filled with the knowledge of the glory of the Lord as the waters cover the sea."

Now that Boreham's pen does its musings in another realm, my prayer is that readers will fill that void for us and probe the simple and the sublime in the strongest sense and the plainest language.

Ravi Zacharias

PREFACE

Second nature, second-class, *second* childhood, *second* best and *second* rate. These are common expressions that we use and hear everyday.

In this book of tasters, *Second Thoughts*, F. W. Boreham discusses five well-known *second* themes—*Second-Hand Things, The Second Crop, Second Fiddles, Our Second Wind* and *Second Thoughts*. It is usual to regard anything that is *second* as being inferior in quality to the first. Who wants to be *second* violinist if you are offered the role of playing first? Who wants to sit in the *second* class carriage if you can ride first class?

However, just as we may speak positively about something that is *second* nature to convey the idea of being completely natural and instinctive, and at the meal table we appreciate the invitation to have a *second* helping, so F. W. Boreham takes several *second* statements and helps us to see their profound worth.

These previously published essays are brought together for the first time. They illustrate Boreham's skill as a wordsmith. Like a jeweller he takes a phrase like a diamond and turns it around to show readers its sparkling and surprising facets.

Frank Boreham said that within the everyday, commonplace things there was a *romance*—a quality that was usually not immediately apparent. He suggested that we all have a responsibility to mine for truths in order to procure 'a nugget of romance.' In his book, *The Tide Comes In*, Boreham illustrated this approach by picturing the way one uses a telescope—by looking through it rather than at it. He said:

"There are two ways of seeing everything. You may see it sacerdotally—seeing, that is to say, the thing itself, but seeing nothing through it or beyond it. Or you may see it sacramentally—scarcely seeing the thing itself, but seeing a world of wonder as you look through it. You never see a thing by looking *at* it; you only see a thing by looking *through* it."

Enjoy reading these samples from the books of F. W. Boreham. Give these essays a *second reading* to experience what Dr. Boreham affirmed, that "life's richest revelations come, not by looking at things, but by looking through them."

Geoff Pound

SECOND-HAND THINGS

❧

Hester Spanton—Auntie Hester, as everybody called her—was the tenant of a large second-hand store and a small asthmatic body. I used at times to think that the adjectives might be regarded as interchangeable. If you had described her as the occupant of an asthmatic store and a second-hand body, the terms would have seemed perfectly congruous and fitting. Her poor little body looked a very second-hand affair. It was terribly the worse for wear, and was so battered and broken that Auntie Hester could only crawl about by the aid of a crutch. It gave you the impression that it had been bought and sold over and over again, and that, having got it cheaply, none of its owners had taken any care of it. I could fancy that I saw Auntie Hester buying it at some dusty old auction-mart, not because she thought that it was strong or beautiful, but just because it was within the reach of her slender purse. Perhaps, I said to myself, perhaps she got it for a song: I have heard of such things; and Auntie was always singing.

And as to the store, it was asthmatic enough in all conscience. As soon as you stepped across the threshold, the boards creaked and groaned beneath your weight. It was a long, lofty, drafty old place; it was littered with the accumulation of ages, and the wind, as it rushed through, touched a thousand queer old things that hung suspended from the ceiling, and set them chattering and shivering. As you edged your way up the narrow lane that wound its tortuous course from the front door to the foot of the gloomy staircase that led up to Auntie Hester's parlor, you felt that everything was in distress. You had to keep both eyes wide open, or, like a dragoon rushing on to an enemy bayonet, you found yourself impaled on the leg of a recumbent dinner-table, or pulled up short by the butt-end of an unemployed curtain pole, or caught by the coat-tail in the fanciful fretwork of an unsuspected bedstead. That path through the store was full of snares and pitfalls; I never breathed freely till I was once more on the street. Try as you might, you could not avoid bumping against disconsolate pieces of ill-used furniture, crazy assortments of rusty ironware, and huge piles of cracked and dusty crockery. If you swerved aside to evade a decrepit old book-case on the right, you knocked down a rat-trap on the left; and, if you stooped to pick it up, you were sure to become involved with a noisy group of fire-irons. And all the way from the street to the stairs, everything that you touched creaked and muttered as though in pain. A wheezy old place was Aunt Hester's store. I heave a sigh of relief as I reflect that, in reviving these unamiable memories, I am but calling up the ghosts of things that were. For Auntie Hester's little second-hand body no longer hobbles about on a crutch; it is at rest. And the asthmatic old store, with its freight of decrepitude; its aches and its pains, its creaks and its groans, is silent too. I cannot think of Auntie Hester without thinking of the green, green grass under which we laid her when her cough had done its worst; and I cannot think of that dingy and cavernous old store without thinking of the red, red flames in which I saw it disappear. A few weeks after Auntie Hester had gone out of the front door for the last time the rickety old place caught fire, and I, for one, clapped my hands as I saw it blaze!

'It reminds me of the Old Curiosity Shop!' remarked Fred Jarvis as we stood together on the pavement opposite and watched the flames at work.

'It reminds me of the Universe!' I replied; and the more I reflect upon that impulsive utterance of mine, the less do I feel inclined to retract it. We elbow our way through life pretty much as I used to edge my difficult way through Auntie Hester's store; and nearly all the things about us are second-hand things. The trivialities of life may be new, or comparatively new; but the big things, the essential things, the things that really matter, are all of them second-hand. This little lamp that sheds its soft radiance over my desk is new; it came straight from the warehouse to my study. But of what importance is this lamp? What would it matter to the world if it sputtered out, never to be relit? But the lamp by which my path is lit all day, the lamp that burns in heaven's eternal noon, is second-hand. None of the goods and chattels in Aunt Hester's store were as second-hand as it. Alfred the Great used it; Julius Caesar used it; the Pharaohs used it; the first man used it as he woke from his eternal sleep and gazed upon the beauty of the world. What, I say, would it matter if this new lamp upon my desk were to go out? But if that second-hand lamp suddenly sputtered out, it would be the end of everybody!

And now, like the image that the photographer sees appearing on the sensitive plate as he washes it in the developer, the principle underlying this matter begins to emerge. If I want a very small thing—a pen or a pencil—it never occurs to me to go to a second-hand store; I send direct to the stationer's, and buy a new one. If I want a medium-sized thing—a house or a shop—I hesitate as to whether I shall buy or build, I weigh the comparative merits of a new one and a second-hand one. But if I want a big thing—a sun or a moon or a star—it never occurs to me to seek a new one; I take a second-hand one and think myself lucky to get it. The second-hand things are the big things; it is the second-hand things that matter. Every morning a second-hand sun shines out of a second-hand sky, upon a second-hand earth, and bids me tread with a brave step life's second-hand roads. The paths along which I shall move have been worn by generations that have dropped into their graves. The language that I shall speak and write is a second-hand language; Shakespeare used it, and even in his time it was not new. All through the day I shall be buying and selling; but I shall be buying and selling with second-hand money; many of the coins will bear the image and superscription of monarchs long departed. And when, at the close of the day, I turn wearily homewards, the second-hand sun will sink behind the second-hand hills; and the second-hand stars will light up the darkness of my night. There are millions of them; none of them were made specially for me; they guided pilgrims across the desert before our civilization began; they marked out a path on the high seas for sailors who have been dead for centuries; they are all second-hand, those stars of mine; they are all second-hand, and they are none the worse for that.

Indeed, I think they are all the better. 'Certain things are good for nothing until they are kept a long time,' says the Autocrat of the Breakfast-Table, 'and some are good for nothing until they have been long kept—and used.' He instances three—a meerschaum pipe, a violin, and a poem. He describes a well-used meerschaum pipe, with its brown autumnal hue. 'He who inhales its vapors,' he avers, 'takes a thousand whiffs in a single breath; and one cannot touch it without awakening the old joys that hang around it—the cumulative wealth of its fragrant reminiscences.' He passes to the violin. Here is an instrument which, many years ago, an eminent old master bequeathed to a passionate young enthusiast who made it whisper his hidden love, cry his inarticulate longings, scream his untold agonies, and wail his monotonous despair. In course of time it finds its way into lonely prisons with improvident artists; into convents from which arose, day and night, the holy hymns with which its tones were blended; and back again to orgies in which it learned to howl and laugh as if a legion of devils were shut up in it. And so, by the time that it falls into our hands, its pores are full of music, and it is stained, like the meerschaum, through and through, with the concentrated hue and sweetness of all the harmonies which have kindled and faded on its strings. And coming to the poem, the Autocrat argues that the poem is nothing at all—a mere sound breathed on the vacant air—when we hear it for the first time. But let the poem be repeated

aloud and murmured over in the mind's muffled whisper
often enough, and at length the parts become knit together
in such absolute solidarity that you could not change a syl-
lable without the whole world's crying out against you for
meddling with the harmonious fabric.

But we have descended somewhat. Until the Autocrat brought us down to the level of pipes and fiddles and
poems we were dealing with suns and moons and stars. Let
us leave the pipes and get back to the planets. The principle
is the same. If the music of the old violin is the sweeter for
the pathos and the tragedy that have saturated its soul, how
much sweeter to us must be the music of the spheres when
we reflect upon the smiles and the tears that those spheres
have witnessed.

We are all affected by the law of association. What can
be more significant than our craving for notable historic
sites? The passion may become morbid, as when we rush to
the scene of a crime or pay for admission to a Chamber of
Horrors. Or, on the other hand, it may become sublime, as
when we stand, with heads bared in adoration, among the
sacred sites of the Holy Land. And yet, critically scrutinized,
there is little or nothing in it. It forms a link, a tie, a bond,
that is all; but we are unwilling to let such bonds be broken.
Is it not with some such feeling that I look out upon the
universe? I like to think that those stars are the very same
stars that comforted Israel in the wilderness; I like to think
that that sun is the sun that David saw when he likened it
to a bridegroom coming out of his chamber; I like to think
that that moon is the self-same moon that illumined the
dread horror of Gethsemane! Like those trifles of which the
Autocrat speaks, these vast orbs are all the better for having

been used. It is true that I am living in a second-hand universe; but I like it all the better on that account.

I certainly like this world all the better on that account. I have often thought that it must have been rather embarrassing to have had the world new. The situation of a young bride who has had no experience of housekeeping is positively enviable as compared with the situation of the first man on the planet. He had to find out everything for himself. He must have spent a considerable portion of his time in making experiments, many of them disastrous and most of them painful. Fancy having to find out which of all the things growing about him were good to eat! And then, having divided the edible from the inedible, he had to subdivide the edible into classes. These things are good to eat raw and these are good to eat cooked! These are good to eat in large quantities and these are good to eat in small quantities! These are good to eat as food and these are good to eat as medicine! And so on. I shudder as I think of the ordeal that fell to the lot of the man who had the world all to himself when it was new. I am thankful that these experiments were all made, and these riddles all solved, long before I appeared on the planet. I have inherited the wisdom of all the ages. My world, I am glad to say, is a second-hand one.

When, however, I have said all that there is to be said in praise of second-hand things, it still remains true that there are things that nobody would buy second-hand. Who, for example, would invest in a second-hand toothbrush? There are a few things that a man must monopolize. Those things must be his own. He would not like to think that they ever have had, or ever would have, another owner.

A second-hand conscience is always a mistake, yet comparatively few people go in for a new one. Most people accept the verdict of the multitude. They feel that certain things are right because the crowd applauds them, and that other things are wrong because the crowd condemns.

A second-hand faith is just as bad; yet numbers of us are content to take over, from someone in whom we have confidence, a faith that is well-worn or out-worn. I have a profound admiration for those Samaritans who, on the witness of the woman at the well, went to hear Jesus and then said to her: 'Now we believe, not because of thy saying, for we have heard Him ourselves, and know that this is indeed the Christ, the Savior of the world!' They tentatively accepted her testimony; a second-hand faith is better than no faith at all. But the second-hand faith only fired them with an insatiable longing for a new one. So they went direct to the Savior! And now behold them tossing their second-hand faiths to the scrap-heap and joyously exhibiting their new ones! Why, I wonder, did Jesus tell His disciples to remember Lot's wife? Was it not because He recognized that petrified pillar on the highway as a monument to the fact that a gregarious religion is essentially a precarious religion? She simply went with the rest; she followed the crowd; her faith was a second-hand faith!

Some of us go in for second-hand visions. The Old Testament has a striking and dramatic story of a brave young prophet to whom a vision came. It was perfectly clear, and, with remarkable daring and fine devotion, he proceeded to obey it. But an old prophet, who had lost his visions long ago, assured the young enthusiast that an angel had told him that the younger man was to do the very thing that the vision had forbidden. The young prophet had to choose between his own first-hand vision and the elder prophet's second-hand one. He chose the second-hand one; wrecked his lifework; and perished miserably.

George Whitefield saw the force of all this. In 1738 he embarked for America. In the downs there lay at anchor two vessels, one outward and one homeward bound. The outward-bound ship numbered Whitefield among its passengers; the homeward-bound ship had John Wesley on board. Wesley had looked forward to enjoying the inspiration of Whitefield's companionship in England, and was deeply mortified at finding him on his way to America. After praying about it, he sent a message to Whitefield: 'I asked counsel of God,' he wrote, 'and the answer is that you are to return to London.' 'If the Lord wants me to return to London,' said Whitefield, 'let Him tell me so! Why should He tell Mr. Wesley?' He declined to receive a second-hand vision, and, to the end of his days, he believed that he decided rightly.

I have just witnessed a striking exhibition of the advantage of new things over second-hand ones. I have been reading the autobiographies of the early Methodist preachers. I cannot sufficiently admire the astute statesmanship, the spiritual sagacity that led John Wesley to insist that these men should place their experiences on record. But the thing that has most impressed me is that these old testimonies are all brand-new. I confess with sorrow that I have been at testimony-meetings that reminded me for all the world of Auntie Hester's store! All the experiences were obviously second-hand experiences. There was no spark of novelty, of originality, of individuality anywhere. The testimonies were as much alike as peas in a pod.

I wished that somebody would jump up and say something new—something all his own. But, alas, it was the same old story, over and over and over again. I turn with a sigh of relief from this vast assortment of second-hand things to these testimonies lying on my table.

'I was hastening on to eternal destruction when the great tremendous God met me like a lion in the way,' says John Haime.

'I had a hell in my conscience,' he says again, with a groan.

'I went to my tent that night,' says Sampson Staniforth, 'seeing all my sins stand in battle array against me!'

'In those days,' says Thomas Olivers, 'my conscience stared me dreadfully in the face!'

'I felt,' says George Shadford, who is in some respects the most attractive of them all, 'I felt as though I had been stabbed to the heart by a sword!'

'I found,' he says again, 'the Judgement seat set up in my conscience; and there I was—tried, found guilty, and condemned!'

It is a great thing, a very great thing, to have entered at first-hand into such poignant and profound experiences as these! It is a great thing, a very great thing, to be able to record them with such skill! Few of us know how, with honesty, simplicity, and modesty, to lay bare the inner secrets of the soul. I felt concerning these men as Macaulay felt concerning the Puritans, that, 'instead of catching occasional glimpses of the Deity through an obscuring veil, they aspired to gaze full on His intolerable brightness, and to commune with Him face to face.'

Face to face!

Life at first-hand!

I feel as I leave the society of such men that I am millions of miles from Auntie Hester's dusty store.

The Second Crop

'*Laugh!*' **exclaimed Dan Kirkland,** as he embarked upon the story of his memorable discovery. 'I never laughed like it in my life! And on a Sunday, too! I was fair ashamed to be seen going home from church in such a frivolous state of mind. Yet, the more I thought about what you had been saying that morning, the more inclined I felt to burst out laughing.'

'It must have been something very funny,' I suggested.

'Funny!' retorted Dan, in pained surprise, a cloud overspreading his handsome countenance as he repeated my unwary word. 'There was nothing funny about it, I can tell you! Molly and I were taking life in deadly earnest in those days, and it was the very seriousness of the situation that set me laughing.' I entreated Dan to be more explicit, and I soon found that he was by no means unwilling.

Dan Kirkland and Molly Aitken were just bringing their courtship to its natural climax when I arrived in Mosgiel. They were one of the first couples that I married, and there sprang up between us the intimacy and confidence that is natural under such circumstances. Driving home across the plain, I often dropped in at the trim little farm on the side of the hill, and always enjoyed the half-hour that I spent at the Braeside homestead. Molly was very proud of her scones and oatcake. She invariably apologized, with a pretty blush, for those that she set before you. Something had gone wrong with the oven, or the flour was of doubtful quality, or Dan had called her from the kitchen at a critical moment. Since Molly's spoiled scones were so delicious, I often wondered what they would taste like on some ideal occasion when none of these disasters had overtaken them. But that golden day never dawned. Molly always spread her dainty cloth with a pretty embarrassment that added a charm to the appetizing meal; and Dan and I poked endless fun at her labored explanations. It was on one of these delightful occasions, towards the end of my twelve years' stay at Mosgiel, that Dan told me the story of his discovery. Molly had just walked off with the tea-things; and he and I were left to our own devices.

'Well,' he began, in response to my appeal for more exact information, 'it was—let me see, how long ago was it?' And then, calling to Molly in the other room, he inquired, 'Molly, how old's Jack?' 'He'll be ten next month,' Molly replied.

'Ah, then,' he resumed, 'it must be more than ten years ago: it was a month or two before Jack was born. It seemed as if everything was going badly with us just then. If you remember, the gold fever was at its height that year. Everybody went mad over the dredging in Central Otago. Every morning's paper brought a new prospectus; each prospectus told of wealthy veins of gold just opened up: each new company promised fabulous dividends to enterprising investors. Molly and I had about a hundred and fifty pounds in the Savings Bank: we bought up mining shares and lost every penny. At just about the same time, the barn was burned down, and, a week or two later, two of our best cows died. We were hard hit and we felt it terribly. Molly wasn't able to get to church, or to go anywhere else, just then; and she used to sit at home here and mope. And I wasn't much better; I fretted about things from morning till night, and, sometimes, from night until morning. Then, one Sunday morning—it was two or three weeks before Jack was born—Molly's mother drove over to stay with her while I went down to the church: I hadn't been going for a week or two. And it was the sermon you preached that Sunday morning that set me laughing.'

I inquired as to the theme. 'I'm afraid,' he continued, 'I can't tell you much that you said, but I think I can find the text.' He reached for the Bible on the shelf behind his chair—the Bible that he was accustomed to use at family worship.

'Yes, here it is,' he exclaimed. 'I always keep a bookmark in the place, because it's in the prophecy of Obadiah, and the prophecy of Obadiah isn't easily found, especially if you're in a hurry. But this is it: "*The house of Jacob shall possess their possessions.*" I forget the sermon. I know that you said that a man might merely possess a big estate, and get but little satisfaction out of it, while another man, who knew how to *possess his possessions*, would get twenty times as much pleasure out of a place nothing like so big. You used an illustration about books. You said that a man who had got together fifty books, and read them, would get more satisfaction out of his modest shelfful than the man who owned a splendid library and never dipped into the volumes he had bought. The only secret of real happiness, you said, lies in *possessing your possessions*. My word, that sermon set me thinking. I went away laughing at myself. "Here," I thought, "I've been spending all my time fretting about the money that's lost, and the barn that's burned down, and the cows that are dead: and I've clean lost sight of the only things worth thinking about—the things that are still mine!" I thought of Molly—the best little wife in the world: I thought of the baby that was so soon to be born: I thought of the home and the farm and the cattle: I thought of the health and strength that I enjoyed—I've never had a day's sickness in my life—and I burst out laughing. I believe I laughed all the way home from church. And, when I got home, I made Molly laugh too. We've often smiled about it since.' Molly re-entered the room at that moment and told the story again from her standpoint. A few minutes later I rose to resume my journey to the Manse; and, as far as I can remember, I was never at Braeside again. A few weeks later I sadly left Mosgiel for Hobart.

II

I am afraid that all this would have passed into the limbo of utter forgetfulness but for a letter which I received the other day from Dan. He sends me an account of his silver wedding. 'We both wished that you could have been with us,' he says. 'We still keep the bookmark at the passage in Obadiah; and, whenever Molly's scones are a little nicer than usual, we talk about old times and wish that you could pop in to enjoy them.' It is this pleasant little epistle, to which Molly has added a playful postscript, that has sent my mind back to the sermon on Obadiah. Out of sheer curiosity I have looked up the notes of that boyish effort; but, on examining them, I have felt much as old Mother Hubbard must have felt when she made her historic visit to the cupboard.

One thing, however, stands out clearly. I see that there is such a thing as the *Law of the Second Crop*. Every farmer knows that his fields often produce a second yield; and, in certain seasons, the aftermath is even richer than the original harvest. '*The house of Jacob,*' says the prophet, '*shall possess their possessions.*' They reaped their *first* crop of pleasure when Palestine was given them: they reaped their *second* crop when they entered into it, conquered and cultivated it, saw their own vineyards flourishing on the terraced hillsides and their own cattle luxuriating in the rich grass of the valleys. The same principle operates in relation to every phase of existence and enjoyment. Take, for example, the phenomenon of memory. We reap our *first* crop of pleasure when we actually enjoy a delightful experience: we reap our *second*—and often our main—crop when we reflect and descant upon it afterwards. Some time ago I went on a trip round the world. It was extremely pleasant; but now, as I sit in my chair of an evening and look back upon it all, I sometimes fancy that the real enjoyment of such a trip lies in the memory of it. At the time, there is too much to worry about. One is harassed by the irksome necessity of making a thousand commonplace arrangements and attending to an infinite multitude of troublesome details. But, in reviewing it afterwards, the sordid and prosaic elements—the minor irritations and disappointments—are forgotten, and the romantic aspect of the journey assumes a prominence that was previously concealed. And thus I harvest my *Second Crop*.

Then, again, there is the pleasure of ownership. We like to acquire, quite apart from the uses to which we propose to put our acquisitions. There is a satisfaction in amassing wealth that is altogether unrelated to the gratification secured by its subsequent expenditure. The joy of the miser is the joy of the *first* crop: the joy of accumulating. He deliberately denies himself the joy of the *second* crop: the joy of living luxuriously on his gathered wealth.

It is one thing to own: it is quite another thing to exploit our hoard. Dr. Handley Moule, formerly Principal of Ridley Hall, Cambridge, used to tell of an old lady with whom he was familiar in the days of his boyhood. She lived for some years in very straitened circumstances. Her husband had died, leaving her nothing but a quantity of land in Australia. She wrote to a business friend in Melbourne asking him to sell it as soon as possible. He did so, disposing of everything but one small and sandy plot that was so barren, and so far from any thoroughfare, as to render it unmarketable. On the proceeds of the sales effected, the widow lived for some years in a condition of indigent respectability, having to look twice at every penny before spending it. Then the unexpected happened. The barren little plot on the edge of the desert proved to be rich in precious metal. It was sold for a fabulous sum, and the widow was lifted from poverty to comparative affluence at one stroke. Yet, as Dr. Moule points out, the gold was hers all the time. But until she realized and exploited it, it was to her as if it did not exist. She possessed it all through the years; but it was only when she *possessed her possessions* that the sunshine came streaming through her windows and she tasted the felicity of the *Second Crop*.

We all possess far more than we enjoy: we are surrounded by wealth that we do not trouble to exploit. Gerald Duncannon has left on record the striking experience that befell him after the bank failure that shattered his fortune. 'Before I lost my money,' he says, 'I bought books; after the crash came, I read them. In the old days I bought them as the fancy took me, for the sake of their handsome bindings, for the sake of their steel engravings, or for the pure pride of seeing them on my shelves. After the financial crisis, I could buy no more; but I began to read, one by one, the volumes that I had so idly accumulated; and thus, in one sense at least, I got more enjoyment out of my impoverishment than out of my wealth.' And I remember a story that John Broadbanks told me one evening at Mosgiel to much the same effect.

John Broadbanks had in his congregation at Silverstream an Ayrshire farmer named Geordie Watt. 'When I called on him the other day,' said John, as we sat by the study fire, 'Geordie was telling me that, twenty-three years ago, he bought a piano so that Gwen—his only child—might learn music. The instrument has been in the home all that time, and he himself has never touched it until just lately. But three years ago Geordie lost his wife, and now Gwen has married, and he is left pretty much to himself. A few months ago he took it into his head that he would like to be able to play. He took some lessons, and is getting on famously. "You'd never believe," he told me, "how

much pleasure I get out of that piano during an evening!'"
Like Dr. Moule's old lady with her gold-mine, and like
Gerald Duncannon with his library, the Ayrshire farmer
was reaping his *Second Crop*. He derived a good deal of
pleasure from the purchase and possession of the piano;
he tasted a rich aftermath of delight when he learned to
play it for himself.

Nor need the application of the principle be confined
to inanimate objects like money, books, and musical instru-
ments. We have a pleasant habit of referring to our kins-
folk and acquaintances in the terms of proprietorship. We
employ possessive pronouns—*my* wife, *my* husband, *my*
mother, *my* father, *my* child, and so on. But here again, it is
one thing to claim a man as my friend, and quite another
thing to grapple him to myself with hooks of steel and
exhaust the wealthy potentialities of his friendship. No man
can afford to repeat Thomas Carlyle's poignant experience.
'Oh,' he moaned, after his wife's death, 'if only I could have
five more minutes with her, just to tell her that I loved her!'
He realized too late that he had possessed without *possessing
his possessions:* he had missed his *Second Crop*.

Man has *possessed* his world for countless centuries: but
he has been surprisingly sluggish in *possessing his possessions*.
For five thousand years the world stood almost still: scarcely
anything was invented: few improvements were introduced.
There was no real reason why Pharaoh should not have pursued the Israelites in airships: there was no real reason why
Herod should not have broadcasted his edict by wireless:
there was no real reason why Nero should not have dashed
along the Appian Way in a limousine: there was no real reason why Lord Nelson should not have destroyed the enemy

ships at Trafalgar by means of submarines. Radium and electricity slumbered in the universe before Babylon was built. Powers that have since proved to be almost miraculous were patiently waiting to be harnessed. Man looked round upon his world with pride. His *first* crop of pleasure seemed so rich that he never dreamed of a *second*. It is taking him thousands of years to *possess his possessions*.

It is easy to possess a Bible in the *legal* sense, and even in the *intellectual* sense, without in reality possessing it at all. I may have *bought* it: I may even have *read* it; but unless it has revealed to me the wonder of the divine love, and awakened in my soul a glad and eager response, it is like the neglected plot in which the gold still slumbers.

I stood at a street-corner last night listening to an open-air preacher. He repeated one great evangelistic pronouncement again and again: '*He that believeth*,' he cried, '*hath everlasting life.*'

'*Hath!*' he called, with tremendous emphasis. '*Hath* everlasting life! And what,' he demanded of his hearers on the pavement, 'what does *hath* mean? It means,' he continued, answering his own question, 'it means that *you've got it:* it's yours—your very own! And it's yours—your very own—the moment you believe!'

The preacher was right—sublimely right: and yet— There is only one way of *possessing your possession* of a book: you must *read* it. There is only one way of *possessing your possession* of a piano: you must *play* it. There is only one way of *possessing your possession* of a gold-mine: you must *exploit* it. There is only one way of *possessing your possession* of everlasting life: you must live it! The man who says that he *hath* eternal life, and does not live in the luxury of such spiritual opulence, is like the widow who owned the gold-mine, yet parted sadly with every penny. The joy of conversion is the joy of the first crop; but the potentialities of the life eternal are by no means exhausted in conversion.

SECOND FIDDLES

Once in a blue moon it falls to the lot of a public man
to read his own obituary notice. Mr. Charles Brookfield
closes his *Random Reminiscences* by telling of an interesting experience of the kind. He was laid up at the Isle of
Wight with a sharp attack of pleurisy; one afternoon it was
rumored that the malady had proved fatal; and the evening
papers rushed out the usual sketches of his character and
career. Mr. Brookfield had the satisfaction of lying in bed,
propped up by snowy pillows, and reading these lachry-
mose lamentations and candid criticisms. The latter proved
by far the more entertaining. But the climax of the sick
man's enjoyment was reached when, in the columns of a
leading journal, he was told that, '*though never a great actor,
he was invaluable in small parts.*' Mr. Brookfield used to say
that he regarded that phrase as one of the finest compli-
ments ever paid him.

Some of the world's best work is done by those who, by
no means great actors, are nevertheless invaluable in small

parts. They are essentially *second fiddles*. They have not the
perspicacity to see exactly what needs doing, but, once it is
pointed out to them, they will exhaust all their energies in
the prosecution of the task. They are eager to help, anxious
to serve, grateful to be commanded. They are conscious of
their own limitations. They know that they can never hope
to lead; but, when they find a leader who knows how to
win their hearts, they will show their delight by following
him through thick and through thin. 'Dundas is no orator,'
Pitt once said; 'he is not even a speaker; but he will go out
with you in any weather!' He was a *second fiddle*.

So was Jamie Greenleaf, my old Mosgiel deacon. Jamie
was no great actor, but in small parts he was invaluable.
I never in my life heard him make a suggestion. He had
no more initiative than the chair on which he sat. When
a debate was in progress, he sat bewildered and confused.
His ready sympathy led him to see the best on both sides;
and I have even caught him voting both for the resolution
and the amendment. In such an atmosphere he was like a
fish out of water. But tell him that, at its last meeting, the
Church had decided on such and such a policy, and that
somebody would be needed to distribute handbills, or run
a message, or visit a distant member, or drive the minister
to an outlying township, and Jamie instantly volunteered
his services. Sunday might bring with it a snowstorm or a
tornado, you would always find Jamie at the church door
distributing hymn-books. Was there to be a coffee supper
or a social evening? You would always find Jamie prepar-
ing the tables and stoking the fire. At the Sunday School
picnic it was always Jamie who pitched the tent, hung the
swings, and kept things merry. If any special service was

approaching—a wedding, a funeral, a mission, or an anniversary—Jamie always gave a 'cry roon' at the Manse the night before to see if there were any odd jobs that he could attend to. If you suggested that he should make a speech, he looked terrified; he could not initiate a policy to save his life; yet I doubt if any one in the Mosgiel Church was held in greater affection than was he. In every club, school, society, and congregation you will find people of this fine type. They are essentially *second fiddles*. Never great actors, they are simply invaluable in small parts.

The cynic will say with a sneer that a *second fiddle* is a *second* fiddle because it cannot be a *first*. It might just as truly—perhaps more truly—be said that a *first fiddle* is a *first* fiddle because it cannot be a *second*. The most striking illustration of this phenomenon occurs in the political history of the nineteenth century. During the memorable period to which I refer, Gladstone was the first fiddle of the Liberals and Disraeli was the first fiddle of the Conservatives. But, at the beginning, the two men were members of the same party. And, as you read Lord Morley's stately chapters, or any other history of the mental evolution of the two men, you are unable to resist the conviction that they were driven into hostile camps by their utter lack of affinity. Each got on the other's nerves; each felt an unconquerable animosity for the other. Had they continued in the same party, one would have had to be *first* fiddle and the other *second*. It was out of the question. Neither could be *second fiddle* to the other; the idea was preposterous, inconceivable, absurd. And so, beneath the commanding influence of their gigantic personalities, parties were remodeled; the one went to the one side of the House, and the other to the other; and they remained protagonists to the end of the chapter. They stand for all time as a classical exemplification of the fact that, while some men are *second fiddles* because they can't be *first*, others are *first fiddles* because they can't be *second*.

Some people, on the other hand, are shaped by destiny to be *second fiddles*. It is as *second* fiddles that they shine. They are second, not because they cannot force their way to a leading place, but because they recognize that they can do their best work in a subordinate role. It has been said that Nelson could never have won the battle of Trafalgar but for the assistance and support that he received from Cuthbert Collingwood. On the day that determined the destinies of Europe, Nelson himself was lost in admiration of the heroic part played by his second-in-command. Collingwood, on the *Royal Sovereign*, led the lee line of ships towards the enemy's fleet, and, first under fire, opened the historic engagement. 'See,' cried Nelson, pointing to his colleague's vessel as she steered straight for the enemy's line, 'see how that noble fellow Collingwood carries his ship into action!' Let us grant for the sake of argument that, without Collingwood, Nelson could not have destroyed Napoleon's fleet that day. But nobody will deny that, if Nelson had not been there, Collingwood would never have destroyed it. The day was decided by the dazzling genius of 'the greatest sailor since the world began.' As soon as the French and Spanish admirals saw the formation of the British lines, they knew that, notwithstanding the superior size, strength, and numbers of their own ships, the battle could end only in one way. They were defeated before a shot was fired. Grant, therefore, as everybody will grant, that Collingwood could not have won the battle without Nelson; and grant, for the sake of argument that Nelson could not have won the battle without Collingwood, and you have only proved that some people are essentially *first fiddles*, and others, just as essentially, *second fiddles*. Collingwood was equipped with every qualification for becoming a *second fiddle*. As a *second fiddle* he was literally invaluable; as a *first fiddle* he would have whelmed a continent in appalling disaster.

Or if, preferring to see the same principle at work in less warlike surroundings, the student cares to shift the scene, he will find an identically similar illustration in the cases of Martin Luther and Philip Melancthon. Luther could never have brought the reformation into being but for the work and influence of Philip Melancthon; and, most certainly, Melancthon could never have done it without Luther. Luther was a *first fiddle;* who can imagine him *second?* Melancthon was a *second fiddle;* he had neither the desire nor the ability to be a *first.*

Everything depends upon the correct arrangement of the first and second fiddles. When, as in the case of Bright and Cobden, the men fit into their right positions at the start, the cause they represent is given an incalculable advantage. When, as in the case of Burke and Wills, the Australian explorers, the *second fiddle* is given first place and the *first* second, the situation can only end tragically. Wills was a born leader; it was the one qualification that Burke lacked. Macaulay has shown that, when Sir James Mackintosh was *first* fiddle and Charles Fox *second,* the Whig cause lost ground every day; but when they changed places it swept the country. There are men who make excellent lieutenants but poor captains; they are admirable assistants but execrable leaders. They are sent into the world to be *second fiddles*.

We ministers are specially sensitive at this point. We are generally regarded as *first fiddles*. Our position involves us in a prominence that is out of all proportion to the value of our service. Every day of our lives we become increasingly conscious that the real glory belongs to the *second fiddles*. The secretaries, the treasurers, the office-bearers of our churches—the people who, year in and year out, cheerfully devote their time, their energy, their wealth, and their ability to the service of the sanctuary—the people who, in many cases, bore the burden of responsibility before we ministers appeared, and will continue to bear it after we have vanished—how could the Church exist without these? They are the pride and the comfort of every minister and of every congregation.

And what of the people who are quaintly termed 'the local preachers'? Consult the records of any congregation in Australia or New Zealand, and, before you have turned many pages, you will find yourself reading the annals of a time when a few devout souls met in a barn or a kitchen and received gratefully the ministrations of earnest lay people whose hearts had been divinely touched and whose lips had been divinely opened.

In the early history of every church there were the gravest difficulties to be encountered and the fiercest prejudices to be overcome. In the nature of things, there were no ministers on the scene, and the positions were bravely and cheerfully taken by busy people—farmers, smiths, clerks, shopkeepers—who, although deeply conscious of their scanty equipment and meager qualifications, were of faith so fine and sense so sound that no discouragement ever damped their ardor and no opposition ever daunted their determination. When the Churches look proudly round at their prosperity, and joyously recount the mercies that have crowned past years, they do but advertise their base ingratitude if they omit an eloquent allusion to the priceless spirits of these valiant men.

I am very fond of Richard Jefferies. My old friend, J. J. Doke, who laid down his life pioneering in Rhodesia, once advised me to sell the clothes from my back, if need be, in order to possess myself of *Field and Hedgerow* and the other treasures that our great naturalist has left us. My only sorrow, as I have read these classics of the countryside, has been that Jefferies hated churches and ministers. He turned his back on a church whenever he caught sight of it, and loved to look out upon the sea because there, he said, he could be sure that the horizon would be disfigured by no steeple. Yet even Jefferies found it impossible to withhold his admiration from the local preacher. In his *Wild Life in a Southern County,* he describes the varied phenomena of a Sussex hamlet. And how can he honestly portray the moving panorama of village life without making some reference to the cottage meeting? He pictures the quaint little room— its old-fashioned furniture and odd assortment of books. There is a Bible among them. Hardly a cottager, Jefferies says, is without his Bible. And no man can interpret that cottage Bible like the local preacher. 'The good man has been laboring in the hayfield from dawn till dusk; but at night he faces without any sign of weariness the devout folk who gather to hear him. He opens the Bible, and, though he can but slowly wade through the book, letter by letter, word by word, he has caught the manner of the ancient writer and expresses himself in an archaic style not without its effect. There is no mistaking the thorough earnestness of this cottage preacher; he believes what he says; no persuasion, rhetoric, or force could move him one jot. Men of this kind won Cromwell's victories; but today they are mainly conspicuous for upright and irreproachable moral character, mingled with some surly independence; such men are not paid, trained, or organized; they labor from good will in the cause.' Thus Richard Jefferies, scorning the Churches, doffs his cap to the local preacher. I range myself, bare-headed, beside him, and am grateful to have found another point of kinship with a teacher to whom I owe so much.

I once preached a long series of sermons on *Second Fiddles*. I could not help it. Paul makes so much of them. At the end of his very greatest letter he devotes a whole chapter to *Second Fiddles*. 'I commend to you our sister Phoebe,' he says; and then he goes on to a long list of people who, none of them great actors, were all of them invaluable in small parts. Take Phoebe herself. In days when travelling was particularly hazardous, when means of locomotion and postal services were unknown, she, a woman, carried Paul's letter all the way from Corinth to Rome. Only a *first* fiddle could have written the *Epistle to the Romans;* but how would that epistle have benefited the people to whom it was addressed unless a *second* fiddle had risked her life to deliver it? 'Paul had a multitude of noble qualities,' says William Brock, 'and he had one quality which great people do not always exhibit; he never forgot a kindness, and never forsook a friend.' And everybody knows why. It was because Paul had sat at the feet and caught the spirit of One who takes good care that no cup of cold water given in His name misses its reward. To Him the players of small parts—the *Second Fiddles*—are precious beyond price.

Our Second Wind

The old road glories in a constant lover. She hates the trier, the taster and the trifler. She scorns to be taken on probation. She dearly loves the through passenger. She likes those who are going all the way. She never yields her best to those who merely dally with her. Her charms are not the charms of the flirt or the coquette. She abandons herself to those who, like Caesar in the Old World and Cortes in the New, burn their bridges and their boats behind them, leaving themselves no loophole for retreat. The temptation of the road is to give up. Weariness becomes intolerable. The romance of starting wears off; the romance of finishing seems remote. We are tempted to abandon the quest. We say with the lotus-eaters:

> Surely, surely, slumber is more sweet than toil, the shore
> Than labor in the deep mid-ocean, wind and wave and oar;

Oh, rest ye, brother mariners, we will not wan-
der more!

It is just at this point that Professor William James, the
eminent psychologist, with his gospel of the *Second Wind,*
is an infinite comfort to us. Professor James says that there
comes a time, in almost everything, at which weariness
reaches the point of absolute exhaustion. It really seems
that we have no option but to give up. We keep on, however, and, to our surprise, find *our second wind.* And, thus
reinforced, we set off again and are able to do more in the
strength of our *second* wind than we did in the strength of
our *first.* That is a very helpful philosophy.

I

The finest definition of the phenomenon of the *second wind*
occurs in Mr. Stewart White's *Blazed Trail.* He describes his
hero's march through the forest with the Indian. The Indian
walked in front. Thorpe followed blindly. Thorpe became
fascinated in watching, hour after hour, the easy, untiring
lope of his companion. There was never the slightest varia-
tion in speed or stride. It was as though the Indian were
made of steel springs. He never appeared to hurry; but neither did he rest. After three hours, Thorpe began to weary.
He felt that he must drop. A little later the aching became
intolerable. 'Then, suddenly, he gained his *second wind.* He
felt better and stronger and moved more freely. For *second
wind* is,' says Mr. White, 'only to a very small degree a question of breathing power. It is rather the response of the vital
forces to a will that refuses to heed their first grumbling

protests.' Here, then, we have Professor James's excellent gospel illumined by Mr. Stewart White's no less excellent definition. Our *second wind,* if you please, is *the response of the vital forces to a will that refuses to heed their first grumbling protests.* This gives us something to go upon.

The Duke of Wellington used to say that British soldiers were no braver than Frenchmen, but they could be brave *five minutes longer.* And it was that *five minutes longer* that made all the difference. I remember that, as a boy, I used to attend a Saturday afternoon Bible class. The morning was spent at cricket or in a ramble on the road. Then came a hearty dinner and a walk to the class. The class was held in a close and stuffy schoolroom. The result was inevitable. Oh, the struggle to keep awake! As soon as we settled down to the lesson that insufferable sleepiness crept over me. And, as it happened every week, I came in course of time to analyze and compare my wretched and shameful experiences. And I found that I arrived quite regularly at a point at which it seemed a physical impossibility to keep awake any longer. There seemed to be nothing for it but to yield. But I discovered, too, that if I set my teeth and made a gallant stand, a supreme effort, a final struggle just at that critical stage, the very intensity of the struggle restored to me all my wayward powers, and, like a train suddenly emerging from a tunnel, I was 'all there' once more. It seemed a horrible and ridiculous thing at the time, but the memory of it has often helped me since. When I am most of all inclined to surrender, I remember Wellington and try to be brave five minutes longer. When the weariness becomes insupportable, and I feel that I must abandon myself to slumber and take my ease, I remember the old Bible-class days in Kent.

II

There are few things in all Bunyan's tremendous allegory more subtly significant than the meeting with Atheist. When he heard that Christian and Hopeful sought the Celestial City, he laughed with a very great laughter, declaring that there was no such place.

'When I was at home in my own country,' he said, 'I heard as you now affirm, and, going out in quest, have been seeking this city this twenty years. I laugh to see you on so *tedious a journey!*'

And so, because of the tedium of the way, he gave it up after twenty years of pilgrimage! And the spot at which he gave it up and turned back was almost within sight of the Celestial City! If only he had been brave five minutes longer!

Now, the world's most distinguished workers divide themselves into three classes.

1. There are those who, like the inventor, do *extraordinary* things.
2. There are those who, like the poet or the composer, do *ordinary* things in an *extraordinary* way.
3. And there are those who do quite *ordinary* things in a quite *ordinary* way, but, because of their indomitable persistency, they do those things on a quite *extraordinary* scale.

The genius of this third class expresses itself in the fact that they keep on after other people would have given up. What did Columbus do, for example? He sailed in a ship, that was all! Many a mariner had done the same before, but no man had held on a westward course so obstinately, so persistently, or so long. We recall Joaquin Miller's fine lines:

> Behind him lay the gray Azores
> Behind the gates of Hercules;
> Before him not the ghost of shores,
> Before him only shoreless seas.
> The good mate said, "Now must we pray,
> For lo! the very stars are gone!
> Brave Admiral, speak! what shall I say?"
> Why, say: "Sail on! Sail on! and on!"
>
> They sailed and sailed as winds might blow
> Until at last the blanched mate said:
> "Why, now not even God would know
> Should I and all my men fall dead.
> These very winds forget their way,
> For God from these dread seas is gone.
> Now speak, brave Admiral, speak and say—"
> He said: "Sail on! Sail on! and on!"

The mate and the men on that little ship were brave, but Columbus was able to maintain his courage five minutes longer, and discovered America in consequence. He did a very commonplace thing; but he did it with more persistence than others were prepared to show.

The same is true of Livingstone. Livingstone walked, that was all. We have all walked, but we have not stuck to it. Livingstone walked, and kept on walking. He kept on walking after he was tired to death of the trudge; he kept on walking after every sinew was cracking from sheer exhaustion; he kept on walking after his body had become what he himself described as 'a mere ruckle of bones.' He kept on walking after it had become the most excruciating anguish to put his bleeding and ulcerated feet to the hot, dusty African soil. And thus, by keeping on, he opened up a new continent.

But I need not have gone beyond Australia for my illustrations. This great Commonwealth has been won for us by people who simply took no notice of weariness. I always enjoy reading the accounts of those conferences held by the first 'overlanders' when their way seemed to have no end. Think of Hume and Hovell and Boyd, away at the back of the Victorian Ranges. They have set out to find the sea on the south, and, at the end of all their resources, seem as far from the ocean as ever. A drought sets in; they become entangled in wild, desolate, broken country that takes the very heart out of them. The cattle become lame, and, altogether, they are at their wits' ends. They beg again and again to be allowed to return, but each time Mr. Hume implores them to make one last supreme effort to reach the ocean. And at length they gaze upon the sea! Or think of Edward Eyre and his tremendous tramp across the continent from east to west. Three days across the burning sands without a drop of water, the horses almost mad with thirst! Again, five days across the sands without water, the horror of it almost insupportable. 'Baxter lost hope, and wished Eyre

to return; but the leader knew only one word—Forward!'
There is nothing in the whole romantic history of exploration more thrilling than Eyre's dire and pitiful extremity
after Baxter had been murdered and all the blacks, save one
boy, had deserted him. Reduced to a skeleton, and almost
at his last gasp, he suddenly sighted a vessel out at sea—a
French whaler. Captain Rossiter took the exhausted path-
finder on board, and would have carried him to his next
port. But Eyre was horrified at the idea. He would accept
only a few days' hospitality. Then, refreshed, he insisted
on being set down exactly where he had been picked up,
and, turning his face once more to the west, he heroically
finished his tramp.

Australia cherishes, too, one romantic record of epic
failure. The Burke and Wills expedition perished through
turning back almost within sight of safety. If only those
gallant explorers had been brave five minutes longer! After
their famous dash across the continent, and their pathetic
disappointment at finding their camp at Cooper's Creek
evacuated, they staggered across the sands towards Mount
Hopeless. Had they gone a mile or two further they would
have seen the friendly smoke of the chimneys of the homestead. They turned back and died in the desert!

III

The road, I said, dearly loves a constant lover, and it is
the glory of the highway that its dust has been pressed by
earth's most dauntless souls. 'No person, having put their
hand to the plough, and looking back, is fit for the kingdom of God.'

'Not fit for the kingdom of God!'—that is a great and a hard saying, 'Not fit for the kingdom of God!' And, indeed, when I come to think of it, I remember that the kingdom of God on the earth has been established by people who, like Columbus and Livingstone, Hume and Eyre, never looked back. I used to think that there was something repulsive about Francis Xavier's notable decision on the Pyrenees. He had set out, after his conversion, to win the world for Christ. In the course of his journey to India he reached the neighborhood of his own home. Entering a rich and fertile valley, the rays of the setting sun shone upon the turrets of a noble castle.

'What a lovely spot!' said Mascarenas, the Portuguese ambassador, who was of the party. Then suddenly stopping, he exclaimed: 'Why, surely, Father Francis, we must be near to your own home! Is not that the Castle of Xavier we see yonder, just visible between the pine trees? You have said nothing, and it had almost escaped my memory. We must make a halt to give you time to pay a visit to your mother and your family!' But Francis Xavier was fearful lest such an ordeal should shake his lofty intention and turn him from his purpose.

'I thank you, sir,' he said quietly, 'but such a visit, and such a leavetaking, would be productive only of needless pain and useless regrets. It would be a looking back after having put my hand to the plough, and might perhaps unnerve and unfit me for the work that lies before me.'

And so, looking wistfully at the stately old home among the pines, and choking down his emotions, he pressed bravely on. There may have been more than a dash of asceticism in Xavier's decision, but he who knows the story of the ten wonderful and crowded years that followed will find it, hard to condemn him. Those ten years stand simply unrivalled in missionary adventure and achievement. Feeling his frailty that day, he was determined neither to be turned aside nor turned back.

IV

In his History of England, Macaulay shows that the same peril confronts people in the intellectual realm. A sincere seeker after truth may, through downright tedium, give up too soon. 'It is not strange,' Macaulay says, 'that wise people, weary of investigation, tormented by uncertainty, longing to believe something and yet seeing objections to everything, should submit themselves absolutely to teachers who, with firm and undoubting faith, lay claim to a supernatural commission. Thus we frequently see inquisitive and restless spirits take refuge from their own skepticism in the bosom of a Church which pretends to infallibility, and, after questioning the existence of a *Deity,* bring themselves to worship *a wafer.*' The mind is weary, and so, like a mountaineer composing himself to sleep in the snowdrift, the pilgrim abandons the track just when there was most reason for pressing on.

When dealing either with the muscles or the mind, the will must not take *No* for an answer. The will is king: its empire is absolute: it must remind its subject faculties that there is such a thing as the *second wind;* and the second wind is *the response of the vital forces to a will that refuses to heed their first grumbling protests.* I said just now that the world's very finest work has been done, not by those who did *extraordinary* things, nor by those who did ordinary things in an *extraordinary* way, but by those who proposed to themselves quite *ordinary* tasks and made them *extraordinary* by the persistence with which they prosecuted them. When weariness overcame them, they relied upon *the second wind.*

Now, if that be so, it follows, as the night the day, that the world's best work can be done by ordinary people. I was reading yesterday of a brave little fellow who, after a terrific snowstorm, began to shovel a path through a large snow-bank before his grandmother's door. He had nothing but a small spade to work with. 'How do you expect to get through that drift?' asked a passer-by. 'By keeping at it,' replied the boy cheerfully. Exactly! That is what Robert Chambers meant by his famous motto 'He that tholes [an ancient word for suffers, endures] overcomes.' Perhaps that is what Jesus Himself meant when He said that 'he that endures to the end, the same shall be saved.' Life's choicest prizes are for the plodders. That was the comfort of poor Mr. Feeble-mind. He was very frail. Death did once a day knock at his door. He traveled very slowly, and had, therefore, to travel alone. He was often imposed upon. He was captured and robbed, and several times almost killed. But he kept on. He had firmly resolved on one thing, 'to *run* when I can; to *go* when I cannot run, and to *creep* when I cannot go.' And, as everybody knows, he came at last to the river that has no bridge, but on the farther bank of which the City gleams. 'His last words,' Bunyan tells us, were: 'Hold out, faith and patience!' So he went over to the other side. It is always dogged persistence that does it.

V

There is a French proverb which affirms that 'on va bien loin dépuis qu'on est las'—'one can go a long way after one is weary.' The *second wind* works wonders. One may achieve so much by simply keeping on that I begin to understand that hard saying of Jesus about those who are positively 'not fit for the kingdom of God.'

I remember hearing Mr. Spurgeon use a graphic and telling illustration. 'In the palace of the Doges at Venice,' he said, 'there hang the portraits of those merchant-rulers, and a long line they make. But one space is empty. A black curtain hangs there instead of a picture. Marino Faliero was found guilty of treason and beheaded. His portrait was removed from among the portraits of the Doges of Venice. But the eye of every person who enters the room rests upon that black curtain. It seems to fascinate each visitor. It is remembered when the other pictures, fine as they are, are forgotten.' There is something infinitely pathetic about that black curtain. It reminds me of Lot's wife. It reminds me of the children of Ephraim, who, 'being armed, and carrying bows, turned back in the day of battle.' It reminds me that 'many of the disciples went back and walked no more with Him.' It reminds me of Judas. What a black curtain is there! 'The approach to the Cross is marked,' says Dr. Campbell Morgan, 'by constant withdrawals, until at last the nearest flee, the story of their going being recorded in one tragic sentence: "Then all the disciples forsook Him and fled." ' 'The sight of a man's back,' says George Macdonald, 'is one of the most pathetic things.' Heaven vouchsafe that the untrodden highway may never see mine!

SECOND THOUGHTS

The man who can keep ahead of his second thoughts is
sure of the kingdom of God. But it is almost impossible
to do it. Second thoughts are fleet of foot, and if I pause
but for an instant they are upon me. The ancients were
haunted by a horror of the Furies. The dreaded sisters
were tall of stature; of grim and frightful aspect; each was
wrapped in a black and bloody robe; serpents twined in
her hair, and blood trickled from her flaming eyes. Each
held a burning torch in one hand and a whip of scorpions
in the other. With swift, noiseless, and unrelenting foot-
steps they pursued their wretched victims. No distance
could tire them; no obstacles could baffle them; no tears
could move them; no sacrifices could appease them. What,
I wonder, was the origin of this weird myth? What was
the substance that cast this hideous shadow? What were
the Furies? Each of the philosophers has a theory of his
own; and so have I! Basing my hypothesis upon the firm
foundation of my own experience, I have no hesitation in

affirming that the Furies which the ancients dreaded were their second thoughts. In many ways, indeed, my second thoughts are far more terrible than the Furies. The Furies tracked down the unhappy object of their cruel malice and slew him; that was bad enough. But my second thoughts hunt me down with resolute and dogged persistence, and, leaving me unhurt, they snatch my children from my arms and dash them to pieces before my very eyes; that is very much worse. As soon as my children are born to me—the children of my noblest impulses, the children of my happiest moods, the children of my better self—my second thoughts give me no rest until they have completed their dread work of destruction. I have been able, happily, to save a few; but they cannot console me for the lovely creatures I have lost. My fairest flowers have all been shattered, my dearest children are all dead!

In all this I am not alone. Others, to my certain knowledge, have suffered in the same way. The New Testament has a great story of four travelers who, one by one, made their way down the Bloody Pass—the short cut from Jerusalem to Jericho. Of the four I find the third—the Levite—by far the most interesting, at any rate, just now. I have never been able to find in my heart much sympathy for the first. He knew perfectly well the sinister reputation held by that gloomy pass; he knew that the darksome forests on either side of the way were infested by brigands; yet he deliberately took all the risks. He was not the first man in the history of the world, and he was certainly not the last, who plunged along a path that he knew to be perilous, and then blamed the church for not helping him when the thieves had done their worst. I am not excusing the priest;

he must answer for himself. But I certainly think that the first of these four travellers has something to explain.

At this moment, however, it is the third for whom I have most sympathy. I see him journeying along the pass; I see him start as he hears a moan from the unfortunate traveler lying on the other side of the way; I see him turn aside and cross to the road to the sufferer's relief; and then I see him pause! That pause spoiled everything! The instant that he paused the Furies were upon him! His second thoughts pounced upon their prey. When he heard the moan, and turned aside, he really meant to help the man. A generous purpose had been born within his breast. His second thoughts, knowing of its birth, vowed that the noble resolution should be slain. His second thoughts watched their chance; he hesitated half-way across the road; his second thoughts instantly tore the kindly impulse from his grasp; with merciless hands they killed it on the spot.

Now, no man can look on both sides of the road at the same time. If that fourth traveler—the Good Samaritan— had been able to do so, he would have seen not *one* Victim, but *two*, in the Bloody Pass. As he came down the road, he, too, heard a smothered moan. Instantly he stopped his mule, glanced in the direction from which the sound proceeded, and saw the wounded man. The thieves, we are told, had left him half-dead. That is the difference between the thieves and the Furies. Second thoughts never do anything by halves. They utterly destroy their victim. He will never moan again. The beneficent impulse that his second thoughts tore from the Levite's breast lay stiff and stark in the stillness of death by the roadside. The Good Samaritan helped the half-dead victim of the brigands from the ditch on the one side of the pass; and he was so absorbed in his merciful ministry that he did not notice the quite dead victim of second thoughts lying in the ditch on the other. It does not matter much; the poor murdered thing was beyond all human help; yet it would have elicited a certain amount of sympathy for the bereaved Levite if the Samaritan had noticed the body and reported it. His attention was, however, fully occupied; he failed to discover the traces of the second tragedy; and, although somewhat late in the day, I am writing these lines to repair, as far as possible, his omission.

And, while I think of it, it is my duty to point out that the failure of the Samaritan to observe the mutilated body of the Levite's generous purpose raises a particularly interesting and important question. Is a man to be judged by his first thoughts or his second thoughts? Is the Levite who turned aside to help, and then changed his mind, any better than the priest who never swerved from his course at all? A broken-hearted father loves to think, as he lowers into the grave the little casket that holds all that is mortal of his tiny babe, that, in spite of death's apparent victory, the child is still his. The little one died almost as soon as it was born; but he somehow feels that, for ever and for ever, it belongs to him, and that he is a richer man for its coming. Now the question is: Am I entitled to cherish the same sentiment in relation to those noble purposes and generous impulses that my second thoughts tore from my breast almost as soon as they were born? Am I not entitled to some credit for the handsome things that, on first thoughts, I meant to do, even though, on second thoughts, I never did them? I cannot say. The problem is too deep for me.

While we stand here, however, baffled by this uncertainty on the major issue, let us gather up such minor certainties as we can find. If we cannot secure for ourselves the loaf that we covet, we need not refuse to eat such crumbs as are lying about at our feet. And this much, at least, is clear. Most of us are a great deal better than we seem. I happen to know the Levite and the Good Samaritan very well. I do not know what they were doing in the neighborhood of Jericho, for nowadays they both live in our suburb. I have always been polite to the Levite, but there has been no love lost between us. Our relationship has been characterized by a distinct aloofness. But I feel to-day that I owe him an apology. I have been doing him a grave injustice. I have never given him the slightest credit for that high resolve that was so quickly murdered by his second thoughts. Even though his pity came to nothing, I like to think that the man whom I have treated so coldly is capable of pity. Even though his resolve perished as soon as it was born, I like to think that this apathetic neighbour of mine once said to himself, 'I will turn aside and rescue this poor fellow.' I have treated him distantly, and passed him with the merest nod, and, all the while, he and I are brothers. We are brothers in affliction. For his trouble is my trouble, his grief my grief. Have I not already said that, over and over again, my second thoughts have snatched my noblest purposes, my worthiest projects, from my breast and murdered them under my very eyes? The selfsame calamity has overtaken him, and I have shown him no sympathy! And all the while he has been watching me. He has seen no lofty design fulfilled by me, and he has taken it for granted that I never cherished one. He does not know what I have suffered at the hands of second thoughts. If I meet the Levite on my way home this evening, I shall show him a cordiality that has never before marked our intercourse with one another. Having been robbed of my own spiritual children by the worst of all the furies, I must extend a helping hand to an unfortunate comrade who has been put to grief in the same way.

The Good Samaritan, too, I meet very frequently. I saw him helping a lady with her parcels only this afternoon. I see now that to him also I have been unjust. Not that I have failed to recognize his worth. Ever since he turned aside that night in the Bloody Pass, and rescued the wounded man whose chance of life was so rapidly vanishing, I have given him a conspicuous place in my gallery of heroes. He is to me a knight of the most golden order of chivalry. And yet, for all that, I have never done him justice. I have always thought very highly of him, but not so highly as he deserves. I have admired his readiness to relieve the distressed, to succor the fallen, and to befriend all who need a helping hand. But I never realized till today that he only does all this after a desperate struggle. I have taken it for granted that he enjoys a complete immunity from the attacks of second thoughts. But I see now that I have been mistaken. When he paused in the lane, as the Levite paused before him, a gang of second thoughts sprang upon him, and attempted to strangle the kindly thought which had been born within him. But he fought for his purpose so bravely, so tenaciously, and so successfully, that the second thoughts were scattered, the generous purpose preserved, and the heroic deed actually accomplished. When I meet the Good Samaritan in our suburban streets, I shall raise my hat to him more reverently than ever. I always thought that he was good; I see now that he is even better than he seemed.

Second thoughts were designed to be the peers of the intellectual realm. They constitute a House of Lords, a chamber of review. It was intended that they should be a check upon any hasty and injudicious legislation that my first thoughts might introduce. And, to do them justice, they often serve me excellently in that very way. My first thoughts are often moved by sentiment, by caprice, by anger, or by some gust of passion; and it is a happy circumstance for me that the project has to run the gauntlet of the Upper House. My second thoughts make short work of such rash and ill-considered devices.

Many a rash scheme, unanimously and enthusiastically approved by my first thoughts, has been contemptuously rejected in the chamber of review. But, unfortunately, that higher chamber has, in a marked degree, the weakness of all such legislative institutions. It is too cautious. It tends to conservatism. It is not sufficiently progressive. It fails to distinguish between a gust of vapid emotion and a wave of magnanimous determination. And so it comes to pass that it scornfully rejects some of the most splendid enactments that my first thoughts produce. The question of the abolition of the Upper House is always a knotty one. It is particularly so in this connection. Would I, if I could, abolish the chamber of my second thoughts? It is very difficult to say. When I recall the wild and senseless projects from which they have saved me, I shudder at the thought of removing from my life so substantial a safeguard. Yet when I remember how often they have stood between me and moral grandeur, I feel resigned to their destruction. The finer feelings invariably express themselves through the medium of first thoughts; it is the more sordid and selfish sides of my nature that reveal themselves when the second thoughts arrive. In reality, the lightning and the thunder occur simultaneously. But the flash of the one is seen immediately, while the rumble of the other is only heard after an appreciable interval.

Conscience expresses itself like the lightning, instantaneously; the mutterings of reason and self-interest, like the thunder, come lumbering along later. It has been said that the men who, in the great war-days, won the Victoria Cross, won it by yielding to the impulses of the moment. Thousands of others were similarly situated, and felt that same sudden and sublime inspiration. But, unfortunately, they hesitated. During that momentary spasm of uncertainty a multitude of second thoughts surged in upon their minds; those second thoughts were, without exception, thoughts of caution, of safety, and of self-interest; and, as a result, the splendid deed was never done and the coveted distinction never won. I really believe that the heroic, the chivalrous, the sacrificial would become commonplace but for the excessive caution of that Upper House.

If ever I become a king, or a dictator, or a president, or anything of that kind, I shall establish a special Order of Merit, to be conferred upon men and women who contrive to conquer their second thoughts whenever their second thoughts threaten the realization of their best selves. The badge of the Order will consist of a representation of the Good Samaritan. And its membership will include some very knightly spirits. I shall confer the ribbon of my Order on men of the stamp of William Law. William Law—who afterwards wrote a book that changed the face of the world—was once a poor young tutor in the household of the Gibbons of Putney—the household that afterwards gave to the world its greatest historian. In those days Mr. Law used to think a great deal about the widows and orphans whom he had known so well, and helped so often, at his old home at King's Cliffe. 'If,' he used to say to his new friends at Putney, 'if only I were a rich man, those poor women and children should never again have need to beg for bread! But it was no good saying '*if*.' He was *not* rich; he was scarcely less poor than the people he pitied. One day, however, he had occasion to visit the city. Standing in the doorway of a bookshop in Paternoster Row, looking at the passing crowd, a strange experience befell him. 'A young man, in the dress and with the manners of a gentleman's servant, stepped out of the crowd and asked him if he was Mr. Law. On receiving an affirmative reply, he put a letter into his hand. When Law opened the letter, he found inside it a banknote for a thousand pounds. No name accompanied the note, and, by the time that Law looked up from the letter, the messenger had vanished. Before Law stepped from that doorway he made his resolution. He took the first coach to King's Cliffe, and, before he returned to Putney, had made arrangements for the erection and endowment of a residential school for fourteen poor girls.' William Law knew that the whole pack of second thoughts were on his track. He determined at any cost to keep ahead of them; and he succeeded so well that upon him I shall certainly confer the ribbon of my Order.

It will be said, I know, that I am too severe. I am indulging, I shall be told, not in a criticism, but in a diatribe. In my fierce reprobation of second thoughts I have almost stooped to invective. I know; I know! But let it be remembered, in extenuation of my offence, that I am a minister of the everlasting gospel. And no man is so harassed and cheated and victimized by second thoughts as a minister of the gospel. Every Sunday of my life I preach a story that might move a statue to tears. It is the story of the Cross; the story of redeeming love; the greatest, sublimest love-story ever told. And I can see, as I watch the play of emotion on the faces of my hearers, that I have swayed their reasons, touched their consciences, and almost won their hearts. But it all comes to nothing. They pause for just a moment, as the Levite paused in the middle of the road. Their hearts are almost won—almost, almost, *almost!* But, while they hesitate, the second thoughts come surging in. I see the millions of them—swarming into the building while the congregation is singing the closing hymn. They get to work without a second's delay. The heavenly aspiration that I marked upon the people's faces is stifled at its birth. The doors open and the crowd melts away. I have been robbed by second thoughts of the fruit of all my labors. If the people had only acted as the Good Samaritan acted, as the hero of the battlefield acted, and as William Law acted, they would have flocked to the Cross like doves to their windows. The man, I say again, who can keep ahead of his second thoughts is sure of the kingdom of God.

ABOUT THE COVER

How does one visually portray words? It is a challenge
with each cover.

To depict the word "second," we used the hands of
a grandfather clock on the back cover. I grew up around
these lovely works of art—in addition to a full-sized one
in our living room, we had a small old-fashioned clock on
the fireplace mantel in the kitchen. Aside from the elegant
outward design, there was a beauty in the hands and the
Roman numeral face. The latter is what came to mind as I
thought about the seconds kept by timepieces.

Cover designer Laura Zugzda was drawn to the image
of the glasses on the open book. It reminded her of time
spent journaling, and how God speaks through that pro-
cess. Removing glasses, pausing to reflect, provides time
for "second thoughts" or simple revelations.

As Geoff Pound writes in the preface, "Frank Boreham
said that within the everyday, commonplace things there
was a *romance,* a quality that was usually not immediately

apparent." "I really believe this to be true," Zugzda writes, "and have experienced this in profound ways through some of the simplest things in my life. There is a truth, a lesson, a beauty, in everything, no matter if it comes in a good way or something difficult. When you walk with the Lord, there is always something new to discover."

A pair of glasses on an open book, a person on a lake at the end of day, and the hands of time, give a sense of thought. This is our attempt to show "Second Thoughts."

Michael Dalton

BIBLIOGRAPHY

SECOND-HAND THINGS: F. W. Boreham, *The Home of the Echoes* (London: The Epworth Press, 1921), 11-23.

THE SECOND CROP: F. W. Boreham, *A Tuft of Comet's Hair* (London: The Epworth Press, 1926), 52-62.

SECOND FIDDLES: F. W. Boreham, *Nest of Spears* (London: The Epworth Press, 1927), 85-93.

OUR SECOND WIND: F. W. Boreham, *The Passing of John Broadbanks* (London: The Epworth Press, 1936), 156-167.

SECOND THOUGHTS: F. W. Boreham, *The Home of the Echoes* (London: The Epworth Press, 1921), 61-73.

Biographies
of Referenced
Personalities

Baxter, John (d. 1841) was a fellow explorer with E. J. Eyre on his crossing of Australia's Nullarbor Plain. When the party was low on supplies and in desperate need of water, Baxter was murdered by two of the group, who then left only Eyre and an indigenous Australian called Wylie to complete the hazardous journey.

Boyd, Benjamin (1796–1851) English-born pioneer and explorer of Australia.

Bright, John (1811–1889) Quaker, was a British Radical and Liberal statesman. He was one of the greatest orators of his generation.

Bunyan, John (1628–1688) Christian writer and preacher, who penned *The Pilgrim's Progress*, arguably the most famous published Christian allegory in history. It was written while Bunyan was confined in the Bedford,

England jail for preaching without a license. He wrote about 60 books and tracts, of which *The Holy War* ranks next to *The Pilgrim's Progress* in popularity, while *Grace Abounding* is one of the most interesting pieces of biography in existence.

Burke, Robert O'Hara (1821–1861) was an Irish-born Australian explorer and leader of the ill-fated Burke-Wills expedition, which was the first exploratory undertaking to cross Australia from south to north, finding a route across the continent from the settled areas of Victoria to the Gulf of Carpentaria. The expedition party was well-equipped, but Burke's lack of good leadership is often blamed for the failure of the project and the deaths of seven people in the party, including his own and W. J. Wills.

Carlyle, Thomas (1795–1881) was a Scottish essayist, satirist, and historian, whose work was hugely influential during the Victorian era. His combination of a religious temperament with a loss of faith in traditional Christianity—heavily influenced by German Transcendentalism—made Carlyle's work appealing to many who were grappling with scientific and political changes that threatened the traditional social order.

Chambers, Robert (1802–1871) was a Scottish author and publisher. It has been said that through his publishing efforts, "he did so much to give a healthy tone to the cheap popular literature which has become so important a factor in modern civilization."

Cobden, Richard (1804–1865) was a British manufacturer and statesman.

Disraeli, Benjamin (1804–1881) was a British Conservative statesman and literary figure. He served in government for three decades, twice as Prime Minister of the United Kingdom—the first and thus far only person of Jewish descent to do so.

Dundas, Henry (1742–1811) was a Scottish lawyer and politician. From 1794 to 1801 he was War Secretary under William Pitt the Younger, ascending to First Lord of the Admiralty in 1804.

Eyre, Edward (1815–1901) was an English land explorer of the Australian continent who later served a controversial term as Colonial Governor of Jamaica. He is perhaps best remembered for the remarkable crossing of the Great Australian Bight and the Nullabar Plain with fellow explorer John Baxter.

Faliero, Marino (1274–1355) held high diplomatic posts and was the fifty-fifth Doge of Venice. He attempted a *coup d'etat* in 1355, at the time being Doge himself, but with the intention of declaring himself dictator. This failed action led him to plead guilty to all charges. He was executed and his body mutilated.

Gladstone, William (1809–1898) was a British Liberal Party statesman and one of England's greatest and longest-serving Prime Ministers (1868–1874, 1880–1885, 1886 and 1892–1894).

Hovell, William (1786–1875) was an English-born explorer of Australia. Governor Thomas Brisbane asked Hovell to join with Hamilton Hume to undertake the exploration of what is now southern New South Wales and Victoria in an attempt to obtain more information about any rivers that might run south in the direction of Spencer Gulf.

Hume, Hamilton (1797–1873) was the first Australian born explorer. He is credited with opening up the continent to settlers arriving from Great Britain. His well-known expedition in which he partnered with William Hovell, was noted for its tension between the two explorers as to whom should and would receive credit for their discoveries.

James, William (1842–1910) was a pioneering American psychologist and philosopher. He wrote influential books on the young science of psychology, religious experience and mysticism, and the philosophy of pragmatism.

Jeffries, Richard (1848–1887) was an English nature writer, essayist and journalist. He wrote fiction mainly based on farming and rural life.

Law, William (1686–1761) was an English mystic and writer of spiritual classics. He is perhaps best known for his work, *A Serious Call to a Devout and Holy Life* (1729). Charles Wesley, George Whitefield, and William

Wilberforce described reading the book as a major turning-point in their lives.

Livingstone, David (1813–1873) was a Scottish Presbyterian pioneer medical missionary with the London Missionary Society and explorer in central Africa. He was the first European to see Victoria Falls, which he named. He is perhaps best remembered because of his meeting with Henry Morton Stanley, which gave rise to the popular quotation, "Dr. Livingstone, I presume?"

Luther, Martin (1483–1546) was a German monk, priest, professor, theologian, and church reformer. His teachings inspired the Reformation and deeply influenced the doctrines and culture of the Lutheran and Protestant traditions, as well as the course of Western civilization. Luther's hymns, including his best-known "A Mighty Fortress is Our God," inspired the development of congregational singing within Christianity. Today, nearly seventy million Christians belong to Lutheran churches worldwide, with some four hundred million Protestant Christians tracing their history back to Luther's reforming work.

Macaulay, Thomas (1800–1859) was a nineteenth-century English poet, historian and Whig politician. He wrote extensively as an essayist and reviewer, and on British history.

MacDonald, George (1824–1905) was a Scottish author, poet, and Christian minister. Though no longer a household name, his works (particularly his fairy tales and fantasy novels) have inspired deep admiration in such notables as W. H. Auden, J. R. R. Tolkien, Madeleine L'Engle, and C. S. Lewis.

Melancthon, Philip (1497–1560) was a German professor and theologian, a key leader of the Lutheran Reformation, and a friend and associate of Martin Luther.

Mille, Joaquin (1841–1913) was the pen name of the colorful American poet, essayist and fabulist Cincinnatus Heine Miller. Called the "Poet of the Sierras" and the "Byron of the Rockies," Miller's poem "Columbus" was once one of the most widely known American poems, memorized and recited by legions of schoolchildren.

Morgan, G. Campbell (1863–1945) was a pastor and itinerant Bible teacher in England and America. After D. L. Moody's death, Campbell served as director of Moody's Northfield (Mass.) Bible Conference. He also served as the pastor of the renowned Westminster Chapel in London, ministering there twice: from 1904–1917 and from 1933 until his retirement in 1943.

Morley, John (1838–1923) was an English statesman, historian and author, who penned, among other fine literary efforts, the acclaimed *Life of Gladstone*.

Pitt, William the Younger (1759–1806) served as Prime Minister of Great Britain from 1783 to 1801, and again from 1804 until his death. He is known as "William Pitt the Younger" to distinguish him from his father, William Pitt the Elder, who also served as Prime Minister of Great Britain.

Spurgeon, Charles (1834–1892) was a British Reformed Baptist preacher who remains highly influential among Reformed Christians of different denominations, to whom he is still known as the "Prince of Preachers." Spurgeon frequently preached to audiences numbering more than 10,000—all in the days before electronic amplification. At age 22, Spurgeon was the most popular preacher of his day.

Wellington, Duke of (1769–1852), was Arthur Wellesley, the noted Irish-born British career officer and statesman. He is most famous for, together with Blücher, defeating Napoleon at Waterloo.

Wesley, John (1703–1791) was an 18th-century Anglican clergyman and Christian theologian who was an early leader in the Methodist movement. Methodists, under Wesley's direction, became leaders in many social justice issues of the day including prison reform and abolitionism movements. Wesley's Methodist connection included societies throughout England, Scotland, Wales, and Ireland before spreading to other parts of the English-speaking world and beyond. His influence is still felt today.

White, Stewart (1873–1946) was an American author, adventurer and novelist.

Whitefield, George (1714–1770), was a minister in the Church of England and one of the leaders of the Methodist movement. He was the best-known preacher in England and America in the 18th century, and because he traveled through all of the American colonies and drew great crowds and media coverage, he was one of the most widely recognized public figures in America.

Wills, William John (1834–1861) was an English surveyor who also trained for a while as a surgeon. He achieved fame as the second-in-command of the ill-fated Burke and Wills expedition, which was the first expedition to cross Australia from south to north, finding a route across the continent from the settled areas of Victoria to the Gulf of Carpentaria. He died alone, before completing the expedition.

Xavier, Francis (1506–1552) was a pioneering Roman Catholic Christian missionary and co-founder of the Society of Jesus (Jesuit Order). The Roman Catholic Church considers him to have converted more people to Christianity than anyone else since St. Paul.

PUBLISHER'S NOTE

We are grateful to Dr. Frank Rees at Whitley College for the permission to publish this book and for the practical support given by the College. Permission to reproduce significant portions of this book can be obtained from Whitley College, 271 Royal Parade, Parkville, Australia, 3052.

A portion of the sale of each book will go toward the training of pastors and missionaries at Whitley College, a ministry that F. W. Boreham supported during his lifetime.

The essays in this volume are drawn from books written by F. W. Boreham and were previously published by Epworth Press.

Sincere thanks to Laura Zugzda for the cover design, Stephanie Martindale for layout and Jeff Cranston for proofing and producing the "Biographies of Referenced Personalities."

This is the third effort from John Broadbanks Publishing which aims to publish and repackage the best of Boreham's writings.

Further information about the life and work of F. W. Boreham is available on the Internet at *The Official F. W. Boreham Blog Site:* http://fwboreham.blogspot.com.

Comments and questions are welcome. You can address your correspondence to:

Michael Dalton
John Broadbanks Publishing
2163 Fern Street
Eureka, CA 95503, USA
dalton.michael@sbcglobal.net

Geoff Pound
c/o HCT, PO Box 4114
FUJAIRAH, United Arab Emirates
geoffpound@yahoo.com.au